FOOD FOR LIFE
A COMPILATION OF CONTEMPORARY PARABLES

VOLUME 1

Bayo Falode

"And he taught them many things by parables, and said unto them in his doctrine..." Mark 4:2

"And with many such parables spake he the word unto them, as they were able to hear it." Mark 4:33

FOOD FOR LIFE
A Compilation of Contemporary Parables (Vol.1)
ISBN 978-1-906428-00-6
Copyright © 2007 by Bayo Falode
Cover Design by RTM in consultation with the author

Published by Faithome Publications
P.O. Box 410
GRAYS,
RM17 9EG

Www.faithfeast.com

CONTENTS

DEDICATION

To my father,
David A. Falode, my first inspiration...

To my mother,
J. Olu Falode, who is the reason I am where I am
today...

THE BIRTH

"HE THAT IS BORN OF
GOD OVERCOMES THE
WORLD AND THIS IS THE
VICTORY THAT
OVERCOMES THE WORLD
EVEN OUR FAITH"

1 Jn5:4

FIRST WORDS

We are in the days when God by His Holy Spirit is revealing His secrets to His children. The secrets of God are sometimes hidden in parables. Jesus used parables. These parables - fictitious stories within precincts of the Word of God convey hidden treasures that guarantee the believer's victory in life.

In the following pages, you will encounter a compilation of contemporary parables inspired by God to reveal the secrets of living beyond the ordinary. Reading them will bring you to a point of absolute victory! The victory that overcomes this world *system* is your faith - your actions based on believing God's Word!

As you read, may the same words that have changed many lives bringing joy and hope to them lift you up! *Remember, "Greater is He that is in you, than he that is in this world system!"*

Peace!
Bayo Falode - The Great House, UK

ACKNOWLEDGEMENTS

I am indebted to several people who at various times encouraged me to keep sending *"FAITH FEAST Food for Life"* by email and also to all who contributed to making this compilation a reality. My special thanks go to the members of *The Great House, London.* Without your belief and commitment we could not have come this far! Also heartfelt thanks to Tola Jegede, Reka Musan and Mr. Idowu Oduntan.

To Dr. Albert Odulele, thanks for believing in me and being a pathfinder. Rev. Ola-Vincent, your lessons on life and productivity have been invaluable. My appreciation goes to Moyin and Shade Ojo, for these many years of encouragement, push and support. To my wife, Gbemi and son, David Oluto for the quiet moments I get at home to meditate and think on the Word after the day's run. To all those I could not mention whose love and prayers keep us going, many thanks. I love and appreciate you all.

QUANTITY
NOT
QUALITY

It was a hot day and a glass or two of water would have quenched my thirst. I grabbed the jug ready to gulp. Something hit me. I just couldn't drink anymore. I looked at the one litre jug and the fifty millilitres cup of water on the table. Then I saw it all. The chemical composition of water in the jug is H_2O and that of water now in the cup is also H_2O. Composition, same ...quantity different!

And God said, "Let us make man in our image, like us... And God made man in his image, in the image of God he made him: male and female he made them."(Gen. 1:26-27)

Yes, it's worth repeating, "You are made in God's own image!" The difference is in the quantity and NOT quality. H_2O in the 50ml cup is the same H_2O in 1000ml cup. The quality is same. No wonder He declared,

"I said, you are gods; all of you are the sons of the Most High" (Ps. 82:6).

He walks by faith...that's why you have the faith nature in you. Your father is a conqueror you are one! He's never failed, that's why he said everything you lay your hands upon to do would prosper! The 'son' of a lion may be called a cub he is still a lion.

You are a son. Show your true character! Your father is a specialist in exploits go and do exploits!

I confess

"...and know that I am made in the image and likeness of my Father God. I have in me the ability to function in love, by faith and in righteousness. I have God's nature in me. I will not fail for Greater is He that is in me than he that is in this world system!"

My thoughts

_____

_____

_____

_____

_____

DNA MATTERS...

Towards the end of the last millennium, Dolly the lamb the first cloned animal emerged. The news rocked the world. It was a major scientific breakthrough in DNA technology. Dolly looked exactly like the sheep from which her DNA was obtained. This great advancement proves that if you take a microscopic part of an entity, you will find it contains the same material composition as the 'mother' entity. One hair strand is now a proof that you visited the salon last August.

"And God made man in his own image after His very likeness... male and female created He them." (Gen. 1: 27)

Whether man realizes it or not, we are all "chips of one old block" God's. We are cloned after the Almighty God. God is love. We have the capacity to love in us. He has faith. You can walk by faith. Remember Jesus said, "If you have the God kind of faith, you shall have whatsoever thing you say." (Mark 11:23)

God uses words, so our composition licenses us to use words. That is why what you have been saying about yourself, your work, relationships etc. is what you have been seeing.

If you are born of God, you have been cloned to have what you say. Start saying only what you want after all God says only what He wants.

"*I am made in God's image and in His likeness. I have the God-kind of faith in me. Because of God's nature in me, I have whatever I say. My words will come to pass! Whatever I decree on earth shall stand. So in Jesus' mighty name I declare peace around me and all that is mine. I declare victory in all I do. So will it be as I have spoken!*"

My thoughts

_____

_____

_____

_____

_____

CAN'T COOK, WON'T COOK!

"Can't cook... Won't cook..." was a popular BBC program, where the "Can't cook" group tries to out wit the "Won't cook" group in thirty minutes. While I am not a fan of either, I certainly can't imagine being a "Won't cook!" Many years ago, King Solomon wrote about them...

"The lazy man would not roast that which he took in hunting: but the substance of a diligent man is precious. (Pro. 12:27).

Unfortunately, the same thing is still happening in this generation. Folks "Can cook" but just "Won't Cook!" Many already have the right information, they have prayed for ideas and found solution to their "hunger" but to step out and do it is a "burden" - That's laziness, that's lack of diligence!

Knowing what to do is nothing compared to taking action and doing it!
"Faith without works is inoperative, inactive, senseless and dead!" (James 2:17 Amplified)

You must get to a productive end. Join the champion's league. Take action! Bring those ideas to reality. Step out in boldness. There is nothing to be afraid of this year, because you are not alone. The Greater One in you is with you. It is Him in you who will get it done. Be encouraged and step out, for the Word says, "He who began a good work in you will be faithful to complete it." Cook and EAT!

I confess

"I have the strength of God in me, to do all things. I reject laziness in my life and make a choice to take action always. I work by faith and not by sight. As I step out, the Lord will lead and guide me through. Success is mine in Christ Jesus!"

My thoughts

_____

_____

_____

_____

_____

MIRROR, MIRROR...

"Mirror, mirror on the wall... who is the fairest one of all?"- remember that fairy tale? Mirrors and reflectors have come a long way. There was a time water in a bowl was used to reflect images, these days when mirror dwell permanently in handbags, airplanes, houses and cars. They could be pretty encouraging and sometimes affect our countenance for the day. What you see in the mirror can make the 'perfect' evening out (it can do otherwise too). "Mirror, mirror..."

"For if anyone is a hearer of the Word and not a doer, he is like a man studying his natural face in a mirror.

After studying himself, went his way, and immediately he forgot what he was like. But whoever looks into the perfect Law of liberty AND CONTINUES in it, he is not a forgetful hearer, but a doer of the work. This one shall be blessed in his doing."(James 1:23-25)

Looking into the Word is like looking in a mirror. When you look into a mirror yourself - God's image! When you look into the Word you see who you really are   a conqueror, the Blessed (One empowered to prosper), and the favoured! If you look a little closer you will see you're the protected, the loved, and cared for, redeemed and going somewhere to succeed. See yourself like God sees you!

Grab that perfect mirror! Spend time in the Word! Five seconds in front of a mirror will do you no good. You need to spend time there! Wake up everyday, grab the Word and say "Mirror, Mirror..."

I confess

"...that from this day, my focus will be on the Word of Victory. It works for me! As I look in the word, the Holy Spirit reveals my true nature to me. I see myself healthy, I see myself in wealth. I see success, victory and strength, these are my portions and I receive them. I walk in them too in Jesus' name!"

My thoughts

_____

_____

_____

_____

YOUR WORD
IS YOUR BOND

"My word is my bond…"
This was the common phrase used in the stock market till the late eighties. Once a stockbroker says that, he is bound by law to transact the number of stocks according to his words. There is an exchange of equity and cash. The deal is then sealed.

"You are taken as in a net by the words of your mouth; the sayings of your lips have overcome you" (Pro. 6:2 BBE)

Your word is your bond! It is a spiritual principle adapted to make the stock market work. Here on earth, words are meant to bind deals. Just like God's Word is His bond. You are bound to have whatever you say. You are made in His image.

God's word in your mouth brings you the right bonds. Speak words of success. Speak words of hope, strength, grace and favour. Use words! Don't just speak! Get the best deals! Claim the best 'stocks'! Remember your word is your bond. Over to you…!
The lips of the righteous know what is acceptable…
(Pro. 10:32)

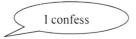

I confess

"...and obtain favour from God and man. The words I speak will come to pass therefore I speak health into my body. I speak favour at work, home amongst peers and colleagues. My needs are met according to the riches of Christ. I am blessed and empowered to prosper!"

My thoughts

_____

_____

_____

_____

LOOK IN THE WORD!

During my driving lessons, I discovered that wherever my eyes went, my hand turned, the car followed. God told Abraham "Look round... as far as you can see that will I give you." He got it!

The children of Israel chose what they saw, "we are like grasshoppers in our own eyes and in their sight...we can't make it!" They didn't! Joshua and Caleb made the same trip, they saw differently. "We are able to take the land..." they did. They saw success and victory. (Num. 13:33)

What you see matters a lot. Do you see a room half-filled or half-empty? Do you see yourself a victim or a victor? You can choose what you see. If the world system paints a picture of failure, fear, poverty and sickness around you, counter it with images from God's Word.

Choose words of Victory, success, wealth and health. Where you look and what you see determines where you end up. Your future is in your focus and sight. You are an achiever, a victor! See no evil, look in the Word!

I confess

"My sight is anointed. I see as God wants me to see. I see progress and prosperity comes my way. I see health and vitality. I refuse every suggestion of the enemy to see impossibilities. If God says it I can have it. I will have it! I am able to take over."

My thoughts

_____

_____

_____

_____

ONCE FREE...

The crowd shouted and applauded as the young man was pulled out of the sewer, he had been buried in there ten minutes before the rescue team arrived. Luckily, he was still alive.

"Thank God it's over," whispered an old lady.

"No, it's not over, we just got him out of the ditch, we need to get the ditch out off him," said the fire chief.

"And be not conformed to this world, but be transformed by the renewing of your mind, that ye may prove what is acceptable, and perfect will of God." (Rom. 12:2)

You have been saved from darkness and translated into the kingdom of light. But you must continually remind yourself that you are a success and not a failure, the head and not the tail, redeemed and not under condemnation. Purge yourself free of any condemning thoughts or past shortfalls. Such hinder progress and your relationship with God. You have been set free now set yourself free! *"Whom the Son has made free is free indeed"* (John 8:36)

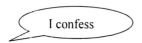

I confess

"That I am free from every form of unrighteousness. I am free from pain, sickness, pressures of life and poverty. Jesus set me free therefore I am free indeed! Free from anxiety, indecision and any mind bugling pressures too. My faith in Christ is established."

My thoughts

_____

_____

_____

_____

GOD'S EVERLASTING WORD

A sudden chill permeated the air and animals began making night calls as skies darkened and an eerie silence swept across Africa all day yesterday (21/06/01). For a moment total darkness reigned in daytime. The solar eclipse travelled for an hour from the west to the east of the continent of Africa. Like one destined to appear the sun made a glorious come back. A new dawn had begun... life flowed again.

"...upholding all things by the word of His power..." (Heb.1:3)

There is no debate here, the Word works! As long as it is called 'day' the sun must shine. By the Word was all things made, by it they are sustained. There may be a momentary reign of darkness but His Word will reign. It will not fail you. As long as there is sun, His covenant with you will remain. It is the covenant of peace - nothing missing, nothing broken.

You can call a party, the Word has said, mourning is giving way to joy! Darkness has giving way to light!

It's time to rejoice so, "Arise and shine for your light is come and the glory of the Lord is risen upon you!" (Isaiah 60:1). Get going, destination ahead…

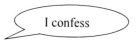

I confess

"…*that God's Word is at work here on earth! His Word is at work in me. It is at work through me and for me! His covenant remains with me and all that is mine always.*"

My thoughts

_____

_____

_____

_____

NO MORE TRIALS AND ERRORS!

Life is too short for trials and errors; we must live with focus and direction. A Chinese proverb says, "It's better to light a candle than to curse darkness."

Even Solomon, the wisest of men tried to find the answer to life. He had the best of instruments and musicians. Then he tried out wealth. In his days, you could pick up Gold on the streets. He then made an attempt with music, food and drinks. It all ended in the loo. Later, he had more than his fair share of women. In his book, we see his conclusion, *"VANITY, ALL IS VANITY!"* (Eccl. 1:2)

You are not born to struggle; make up your mind once and for all to live a life worth emulating. You must not end up saying, "vanity." You need to direction to life, light brings direction. The question of life will only find an answer in HIM. Switch on the light in you. In HIM was life and the Life was the light of men. (John 1:4)

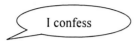

I confess

"that the life of God is in me. I am guided by His light. My beginging may be small but my later end shall surely be great in God. No more trials and errors, by the light of God in me I know what to do always in Jesus name!"

My thoughts

_____

_____

_____

_____

EUREKA!
I FOUND IT!

The pool was warm and relaxing; the little ones swam and played with their toys. One caught my attention, time and again he tried to push the ball under water but it kept popping back to the surface. Just like Archimedes, when he discovered that the apparent weight loss in water is equal to the volume of water displaced, I shouted, "Yes! Found it!"

An inflated ball will float no matter the volume of water - in a bathtub or on an ocean. Why? The pressure inside the ball is greater than the pressure outside.

"Ye are of God, little children, and have overcome them: because greater is he that is in you, than he that is in the world." (1John 4: 4)

Friend we have nothing to fear, as long as the Holy Spirit is in us! We cannot 'sink'. He is the greater one in us! He will cause your head to rise above the waters and pressures of the world. Just increase the pressure within, you

will always rise to the top. Above all issues of life! DON'T GIVE UP! Rise by the strength of the greater One in you!

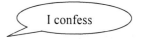

I confess

"That the pressures of the system is below me. The ability of God is in me. The Holy Spirit the Greater One is in me. I will rise above the pressures of my daily walk. I am above only and never beneath."

My thoughts

_____

_____

_____

_____

LIKE FATHER, LIKE SON!

He had been busy all week now things were gradually taking shape. But today He was on a different piece. He knew what he wanted. Minutes later, the carving was finished a masterpiece, the handy work of a skilful sculptor, a great work of art. He glanced at the finished work and then to the mirror he had placed opposite him. The sculpture was what He wanted HIS EXACT IMAGE. Then he broke the long silence. And God said, "Very good."

"And God said, Let Us make man in Our image, after Our likeness...
And God saw everything that He had made, and behold, it was very good. And the evening and the morning were the sixth day." (Gen. 1:26-31)

Friend, you were created in God's image. You are a masterpiece! There is something about you that is like the Maker. You are His image, made in His likeness. When He made you, He put some of His abilities and nature in you:

1. God is a success you are born to succeed.
2. He is a God of faith so you are to have the God-kind of

faith.

3. He is Love you must walk in Love.
4. God uses Words Go and use words.

"And God said... And God saw!" Go ahead; say it and you will see it! You are the image of the Living God!

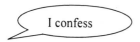

"I am like my Father in heaven. I have His nature in me. God is a success I am born to succeed. He is a God of faith I have the God-kind of faith. He is Love I have the capacity to walk in Love. God uses Words I believe in my words and they come to pass!"

My thoughts

_____

_____

_____

_____

TURN THE 'BLESSING' ON!

"I can't continue like this...Things must change!" So Jabez prayed, *"Oh, that thou would bless me INDEED and enlarge my coast and that your hand might be with me that thou keep me from evil that it may not grieve me" And the Lord granted him his request."* (1 Chron.4: 10)

"God granted him his request!" - I like that. There are two points here:

1.   The word "indeed" means he had already been the blessed (being of the lineage of blessed Abraham) but the effect of that blessing was not obvious in his life.

2.   It was Jabez who determined the time of his change and God granted him the change!

It is one thing to be blessed and it's another thing for the result of the blessing to show. If you belong to the family of the Anointed one, you have been blessed, empowered to prosper, to reach out and to succeed. It must show around you! Lay a demand on it! It must shine!

You see, the blessing is also the anointing; it is like a jacket that has its own magnetic field. When you put it on, it pulls favour towards you. Success comes running after you. Iron fillings have no choice when a magnet comes to town they must be attracted! Good things have no choice but come your way from today. Be conscious of it. Call it to action. You have been blessed and it MUST show. The timing is in your hands turn it on!

I confess

"...it is well with me on every side. Lines will fall in pleasant places for me. From today the blessing of the Lord is released in it's fullness in my life. I arise and shine! My light is come and God's glory is arisen on me!"

My thoughts

_____

_____

_____

_____

WE...WE... We...

Coping with life, business, family or academics could at times be financially demanding. Philip found himself in the same position.

"Where shall 'we' buy bread for these people to eat?" the Master had asked.

He answered, "Well... these cash won't be enough, with five thousand men sitting."

"Except this boy's five loaves and two fishes and that won't be enough." He added.

"Let's have it..." was the reply.

So everyone ate and they had takeaway packs in baskets. Three points to note here:

1.   Jesus had said "WE",
2.   They provided something,
3.   And there was supernatural supply.

Be encouraged, you are not alone, he is with you. There is something you have - gifts, visions or ideas, allow him to use it through you. In there lies the root of your supplies. You cannot be stranded because he cannot be stranded. Your needs will be met!

"*...the Lord is me with in all my daily endeavours. I will not know any lack. He is working with me, in me and through me.*"

My thoughts

_____

_____

_____

_____

THINKING OF YOU

For many years he wondered, since the day Adam was formed. He had looked at the stars, studied the galaxy and did not find an answer. When he could no more contain it, the angel had to ask,

"What is man that you are mindful of him? I mean the son of man that you pay him visits? You made him next in rank to the Almighty and crowned him with such glory and honour. You also gave him control over all that you have made!" (Psalm 8 paraphrased)

You are special and God's mind is full of you. Even angels wonder why? Today, He said to tell you that "YOU ARE IN HIS THOUGHTS". So what are His thoughts, if His mind is full thinking about you all day, what is He thinking?

"For I know the thoughts that I think of you, thoughts of peace, and not of evil, to give you a future and a hope." Jer. 29:11

Yes, God is thinking about your good, He is concerned about your peace. He is thinking of you succeeding and making it to the end! HE CAN'T HELP BUT THINK OF YOU ALL DAY. Read Hebrews 2:6-7

"*God's thoughts to me are of good. They will come to pass in my life. I will enjoy a brighter future. I embrace His plans for me and expect good things to come my way in Jesus name.*"

My thoughts

_____

_____

_____

_____

A PENNY FOR YOUR THOUGHTS

"A penny for your thought, friend," he said noticing the quietness in the car.

"Sorry, I am worth much more than that..." I smiled.

Having provoked his thought, I added, *"For as a man thinks in his heart, so is he..."* (Pro. 23: 7)

You are a product of your thought. What are you thinking? If I can value your thoughts, then I can tell you your worth. Some thoughts are not worth more than a penny. Others are productive and invaluable. Like God's. His thoughts are deep and its worth and results immeasurable. Hear the Psalmist declare...

"O LORD, how great are your works! And your thoughts are very deep." (Ps. 92:5)

Now you are a product of His thought. How encouraging! The Word says you have the mind (the thought generating center) of Christ. You can think like him. Renew your mind by the Word then your thoughts will become deep and your works great. There is an edge we have over the world system we have been equipped with a sound mind. It is a productive mind. Put it to work! Unlock this priceless wealth in you. Go above the penny-thought level. Change your worth!

I am glad the Word says, *"God will do far above that which we can ask or think!"* (Eph. 3:20)

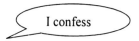

I confess

"My thoughts are great. I have a sound and productive mind. The mind of Christ is mine. God is at work in my mind shaping my world positively. He is doing far above my request and much more than I think. My thoughts are positive!"

My thoughts

_____

_____

_____

_____

THE LIFE

"...AND THAT LIFE I NOW LIVE IN THE FLESH, I LIVE BY FAITH TOWARD THE SON OF GOD, WHO LOVED ME AND GAVE HIMSELF ON MY BEHALF."

GAL 2:20

"THE JUST SHALL LIVE BY HIS FAITH"

Hab 2:4

SEE THE END FROM THE BEGINNING...

Maria climbed up the ladder, a bucket of paint in hand as she struggled to maintain balance but made it to the top. Then she found out the ladder was resting on the wrong side of the wall. So she came all the way down with the paint in hand and did it right.

If you don't know your destination you will never know when you get there. After that God had made the earth, fish, herbs and all things, He said "it was good." Then when He made man he said "VERY GOOD!" You see, He knew what He wanted and knew when he finished. He began with the end in mind! (Genesis 1:1-end)

"I alone am God... no one is like me. Think about what happened many years ago. From the very beginning, I told what would happen long before it took place. I kept my word" Isaiah 46:9 10

Beginning with the end in mind does two things:
(1) It helps you know where you're going;
(2) It shows you where you are now so that the steps you take are always in the right direction.

I confess

"...I am clear about my life goals. I will not be confused. My path is bright and clear. May the Lord grant me foresight to see ahead and lead me in the right direction in Jesus' name."

My thoughts

_____

_____

_____

_____

WHEN SEEING BECOMES BELIEVING

"Seeing is believing…" they say.
"Half truth" I will say. We don't have to see before we believe. You are meant to believe then see it, however there comes a time when what you see becomes what you believe. After all, most of us believe and sometimes expect what we see on the television to happen to us.

Someone rightly said, "What you look at will determine what you see, what you see will affect what you perceive, your perception in turn affects you understanding and your understanding determines your actions."

So, have you been taking the right steps towards your destiny, vision and goals? Can you justify your actions? If not, where have you been looking? The word tells us where to look, *"Looking unto Jesus, the author (who knows the beginning) and the finisher (who sees to the completion) of our faith (trust and believe in God's fulfilment of our dreams and aspirations)"* Heb. 12:4

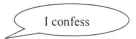
I confess

"...and declare, that my beginning is settled in Jesus and my finishing is finalized in him too. Therefore I declare my trust is in him. He will start with me and end with me. As I journey through life my faith in him is established for the fulfilled of purpose and destiny. Amen."

My thoughts

_____

_____

_____

_____

THE MILLION DOLLAR QUESTION

Even if the much prayed for blessing came in person many may remain bound by past failures in relationships, business or academic pursuits.

There were some folks at the pool side called 'House of mercy', they all needed miracles, and they were expectant.

"Will thou be made whole?" asked Jesus one.

"Sir," he replied, "I have been here 38yrs and I don't have friends to help me... you see I know I would have made it years ago to the pool, but other people are faster..." Well, thank God for mercy personified, Jesus healed him. (John 5:1-10)

Excuses could have cost him his miracle. It's time to move forward and stop dwelling on the past, "I wish I had done this..." or "Had I known...?"

Other people may look smarter or faster; you run at your pace, expect God to see you through - Don't forget He is always by your side, asking the question, "WILL THOU BE MADE WHOLE?" or "WOULD YOU LOVE TO BE HELPED?"

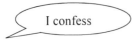

I confess

"That my help comes from the Lord. By the precious blood of Jesus, I obtain mercy in my time of need always. I stay whole, nothing missing, nothing broken. God's mercy endures over me and all that is mine. Glory to God!"

My thoughts

_____

_____

_____

_____

BEAN POTTAGE
IN THE POT....

The pottage was sizzling hot, red and inviting. The aroma had filled the kitchen to the hallway. For a moment it looked like there was nothing like it and there will never be anything like it. Take a look again! It must be eaten hot! It must be eaten now! Now or never! The big decision was made,

"And Esau said, Behold, I am at the point of dying, and what profit shall this birthright be to me? And Jacob said, Swear to me this day. And he swore to him, and he sold his birthright to Jacob.
Then Jacob gave Esau bread and soup of lentils. And he ate and drank, and rose up and went his way. And Esau despised his birthright." (Gen.25:32-34)

He later sought the birthright with tears and sorrow but it was too late. *"...when he desired to inherit the blessing, he was rejected; for he did not find any place of repentance, though he sought it carefully with tears.* (Heb 12:15 -16)
Certain things are not permanent. Such short-term pleasure must never take pre-eminence over choices that will affect the future. Besides, both boys must have been hungry, but Jacob made a choice to delay

gratification for a better future. Your decisions today will affect your position tomorrow.

The choice is yours, are you content with your present status or would you burn the midnight candle for a change? You may have to decide between studying and visiting, or between sleeping and praying. Whatever you choose, make sure it's for a good future.

I confess

"My inheritance is in Christ. My eye of understanding is flooded with light. I receive the Wisdom and spirit of revelation. In Jesus name, I will make the right choices at every turn in life. My decisions will be right! By faith I will be led and strengthened by the Holy Spirit. Amen."

My thoughts

_____

_____

_____

_____

ONE WORD
FOR HARVEST

Farmer Alex retired to the shed. He had ploughed and sown his seeds. Two days later, corn blades began to sprout.

"How did you do that, grandpa?" asked little Amy who had watched him plant the seeds.
With a smile Old Alex replied,
"I didn't do it, I only obeyed a principle. These 37 years, I have learnt that all you need to do is to make contact between the seed and the earth, the earth will see to the production of fruits."

And Jesus said to them, *"Don't you understand? The seed is the Word of God and the earth is the heart of men. "*(Mark 4:14)

Friend, the principle is same. One victory verse from the Word in your heart and the blades of victory will begin to sprout. One word of healing and you will see healing. One seed of favour and favour goes with you everywhere. But there must be a contact between the heart and the Word. How?

(1) Take a verse concerning your issue; plant it in

your heart by meditating or simply put, continuous thinking about it;

(2) Water it by saying it until you believe it in your heart. Once in your heart, give thanks to God, for the heart like the soil, will release forces to see the Word (seed) produce.

See you at harvest time!

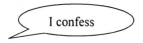

"... God's Word works for me! I am a believer. My heart is receptive. I can understand the things of God and have the ability to produce results. In Jesus name, I am a productive child of God!"

My thoughts

_____
_____
_____
_____

LESSON FROM A LUNCH BOX

It was a 3-day revival conference, over five thousand men in attendance not counting the women and children had gathered to listen to the words of the Master himself. A great need arose, everyone ran out of food. Andrew peeped into a little boy's lunch bag; there were five loaves of bread and two fishes in it. The Master called for it, blessed it (empowered it to prosper), and the little lunch feed over 5,000 people and they had twelve baskets remaining.

"I can do all things through Christ that gives you strength." Phil. 4:13

There are any times our visions and goals appear to be so big, the thought of it makes one feel small. You may feel like a small-little-what-can-I-do lunch in the midst of demands. However you can choose to be a blessing, if God gave you the skill, talent and ability, He will back you up to success.

Hand the visions and goals over to Jesus in prayer. He will bless it and there will be an empowering for success that will rise up in you.

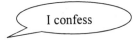

I confess

"... and know that I can do all things through the anointing of Christ in me. I declare I am a blessed child of God and that from this day I am a blessing to my generation. Through me and by my hands the Lord will bless others in Jesus name!"

My thoughts

_____

_____

_____

_____

'SEE BEST BEFORE END'

Ever seen "Best Before see End (BBE) 09/2008 or Expiry date 09/2008" on a tin, drink can, food pack or eggs. Well that simply shows that things do expire. Really everything on earth has an expiry date. Man, birds, cars (Porsches don't last forever you know). But there is something about staying relevant till the expiry date comes. There is just something good in being useful and relevant to your environment as the years roll by. The Word says,

"Iron makes iron sharp; so a man makes sharp his friend." (Proverbs 27:17, BBE)

Benson Idahosa once said, *"If you don't stay around people that will inspire you, you will expire."*

Friend, you must remain relevant. Don't expire before end! Walk with people who talk faith, progress and success in life. Don't share your vision with grasshopper-minds talk to giant killers. Let every Joshua look for a Caleb. "Show me your friend and I will tell you who you are," goes the saying. May I add, "And where you are going."

Read materials on successful businesses, ministries, inventions and champions! When you stop reading you start dying! The greatest of all minds is God's His words are His thought. Read it! Think like He does. Great minds never expire we are still hearing about Isaac Newton and Albert Einstein. So remain relevant!

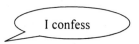

"That through the years to come my life will have a meaning. I will be relevant. The Lord willing, I shall continue to be fruitful even at old age. I am like a tree by the stream bringing forth fruit in the right season. May the Lord continually send worthy people my way to help sharpen his grace, skill and ability in my hand!"

My thoughts

_____

_____

_____

_____

UNKNOWN DESTINATIONS...

As the car cruised on, they knew they needed a saviour. They had never been this route before - it was their first trip to the cities beyond the sea. The route was long, the journey could have been tiresome but they drove on towards their destination with great excitement, expectation and assurance - their 'saviour' will see them through. The saviours did! The road signs did!

"Looking unto Jesus (THE WORD) the author and finisher of our faith..." (Heb. 4:12 Emphasis mine)

No one has ever travelled through his or her entire life; it is like driving an unknown route. But we can reach our desired destinations in style. God's plan is that you get to see your visions, goals and arrive at the desired destination. That's why He gave you His Word! With your eyes on the word, success is sure. Be assured you are bound to arrive!

You may not be there yet, but get excited, let your hopes be renewed; your road signs cannot fail! Keep looking for His leading and you will surely make it!

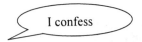

I confess

"That focussed on Jesus, the writer of my life-script, I am sure of arriving at my destination. I am led by God's Holy Sprint. As He leads by faith I follow. Oh yes! My hopes are now revived and surely my expectations will not be cut short."

My thoughts

_____

_____

_____

_____

YOU'RE HIGHLY FAVOURED!

The horse riders stopped abruptly. Their gaze was upon a young slave girl, dressed shabbily and covered in sweat. It was obvious she had toiled all day like others. Their mind was made up she must go! Esther was whisked to the king's palace for a beauty contest. After one year probation period, the curtains rolled. One after the other the girls came in.

According to the Royal Family correspondent, this was what happened, *"Then it was Esther's turn...and the king loved Esther above all the women, and she found grace and FAVOUR in his sight more than all the virgins, and he set the royal crown upon her head, and made her queen instead of Vashti."* (Esther 2:17)

There an edge the believer has a cutting edge, it is called the favour dimension. It lifts you to levels beyond your dreams. When favour steps in labour ceases. It took Esther to the throne. By it Joseph became a Prime Minister. Favour gets the job done! As you go for your business contracts, interviews, to your boss, supervisor or lecturer the same favour goes with you. It will cause the right decisions to be made for you. So friend, get conscious of the fact that you are highly favoured. See you at the top!

"For you, Lord, will bless the righteous; with favour will you surround him as with a shield." (Ps. 5:12)

I confess

"Favour over my life! My beginning may be small but my latter end shall surely be increase. I find favour before God and man. The Lord is setting me up for greater heights. It's a new season for me a season of favour on every side in my life"

My thoughts

_____

_____

_____

_____

TICK SAYS
THE CLOCK!

As I relaxed my mind wound back to my early years of life, I heard voices. Little kid's voices singing the all time nursery rhyme,

> *"Tick," says the clock*
> *"Tick," "Tick,"*
> *What you have to do*
> *Do quick!*

"Things which matter most must never be at the mercy of things which matter least," said Goethe.

When this year runs out how would you like to remember it? Could it be said you walked by faith, believed God to meet your needs, and achieved your dreams and goals for the year in spite of whatever comes your way?

Achievers major in the major things of life while others major in the minors. Every step you make this year should be towards your God-given visions and ideas.

"Looking unto Jesus the author and finisher of our faith; who for the joy that was set before him endured the cross, despising the shame, and is set down at the right hand of the throne of God." (Hebrews 12:2)

" My dreams will come into fruition. As I focus on the author of my faith, in Him I begin and He also will bring it to pass. "

My thoughts

_____

_____

_____

_____

WHERE IS YOUR FAITH?

One day, Jesus and his disciples got into a boat, and he said, "Let's cross the lake." They started out, and while they were sailing across, he went to sleep. Suddenly a windstorm struck the lake, and the boat started sinking. They were in danger.

So they went to Jesus and woke him up, "Master, Master! We are about to drown!" Jesus got up and ordered the wind and waves to stop. They obeyed, and everything was calm.

Then Jesus asked the disciples, "Don't you have any faith?" But they were frightened and amazed. They said to each other, "Who is this? He can give orders to the wind and the waves, and they obey him!" (Luke 8:22 -25)

FAITH believes in something or someone. For your faith to work you must believe that God exists, means what He says and has the ability. In that boat, Jesus asked the disciples, *'where is your faith?'* He couldn't see it.

Today, in spite the pressures around let your faith rest on these three;

1. HIS PRESENCE - He will never to leave you Nor forsake you.

2. HIS PROMISE - Not a jot/speck of His Word to you will go unfulfilled

3. HIS POWER - He is able to do, exceeding abundantly, above all we ask or think.

I confess

"...that by faith that the Lord's presence is with me. He will never leave me he is always with me. God's promises are mine. to me they "YES" in Christ and "AMEN" to me. I have his glorious power at work on my behalf doing far above that which I ask or think. Glory to God!"

My thoughts

_____

_____

_____

_____

EVER HEARD OF GIGO?

Obviously this harvest was no good. Looking over to the 10-acres farmland, Abbey wished he had done better in the planting season like his neighbour Phil. Four hundred miles away, in a software company, Derek his son bangs and swears at his office PC.

"Why doesn't this computer just give me the right result? At least Harry's programme just ran on it…ghh!"

"Check your codes, boy!" responded his team leader. "It's called 'GIGO'- 'garbage in, garbage out!"

"He who deals with a lazy hand becomes poor; but the hand of the hard worker makes rich." (Prov. 10:4)

If you type in 'gobbledygook', you get 'gobbledygook'. Your expected output depends on your input. Would you like to see the fruit? Then labour! "Whatsoever a man sows that shall he reap."

Now don't give up on your dreams yet. I know you had plans laid out in January. It's not over! Take an inventory. How much did you really put in? Your input will determine your output. Every farmer knows the secret of a good harvest is planting good seeds. The Word is like a seed and the heart - the soil. It has the ability to produce the desired harvest. But you must do the sowing. "GIGO" it's your turn…

I confess

"…that am a sower of God's ever productive seed. My harvest is near. God's word cannot fail me! From this day on, I shall l eat the fruit of my labour in Jesus name, Amen."

My thoughts

_____

_____

_____

_____

LIVE AND LET LIVE

Whatsoever men value they use well, and treat with utmost importance. We could live our lives better if we placed values on it. Probably not in pounds sterling nor in dollars. The human life is worth more than any currency. Jesus said *"... a man's life does not consist in the abundance of what he possesses."* Luke 12:15

You have only one life to live - this one. Place a value on it. Don't waste it. The words of Oswald Smith echoes through the ages, *"The great use of one's life is to spend it for something that will outlast it. For the value of life is computed not by it's duration but by it's donation..."*

Your life must count to everyone around you, family, friends and co-workers. Be a blessing in your community, nation and the world. Let it be known that when you passed through you did like Jesus did - YOU AFFECTED YOUR WORLD!

 I confess

"...that through Christ my life shall be a blessing to many. From this day, I become a source of

encouragement to others. I will be a source of joy, hope and a stirrer of faith. Everyone I come in contact with will be encouraged."

My thoughts

_____

_____

_____

_____

THE STAND

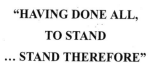

"HAVING DONE ALL,
TO STAND
... STAND THEREFORE"

EPH 6:13

"Above all, put on the shield
of faith"

Eph 6:16

PALACE BOUND

No one knew what was to become of young Joseph, not even the prison officials. His Majesty had summoned him. As he shaved hurriedly, he remembered the past. Bullied by his brothers, sold to slavery for using his gift, jailed for good looks, life had not been fair. What next?

"Could you interpret my dreams?" The Pharaoh asked.

"Ye... yes, I...I can Your Majesty." He finally found his tongue.

It was a direct call on his gift. By now he had become an expert after practising with other prisoners' dreams. So he did the job and also gave the king an outstanding economic and financial plan. Then he got paid for the ten minutes consultation. He became the Prime Minister the same hour.

"Have you seen a man who is an expert in his craft or business? He shall stand before kings and not ordinary folks." (Proverbs. 22:25)

Kings pay better! Experts and professionals will forever be needed and of cause better rewarded.

Consider these three things today:
1. What is the demand for what you are doing?
2. Your ability to do the job
3. How much will it cost to replace you? - Who is easily replaced the Chief Executive Officer or the Clerical Assistant?

BE A PRO! Become the best in your field; give no room for mediocrity and sub-standard jobs. Expertise is much rewarding.

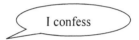
I confess

"...That I shall be the head and not the tail; that by the help of the Holy Spirit I shall be diligent in all my doings, hardworking and seek to give my best always. In Jesus' name my gift will make room for me at the top!"

My thoughts

_____

_____

_____

_____

GOING PLACES!

About four cars branched off to the filling station by the highway. It was to be the last station for several miles. The queue was long. A gentleman slowly approached the station, his groomed hair and well-tailored suit covered with dust. Hanging on his right hand was a keg. He had just completed a non-award winning 4-mile trek from his car.

"They that were foolish took lamps and took no oil with them: But the wise had oil in their vessels with their lamps...And while the foolish five went to buy oil, the groom came...and the door was shut!" (Matt. 25:1-11)

Going places? Preparation is the key. You know drivers who are heading somewhere because they buy fuel! You must be prepared to succeed every waking day. Plan your day, your moves and do what you have to do at the right time. Don't let opportunities slip through your fingers. Grab them! "To fail to prepare is to prepare to fail," goes the saying.

I confess

"By the help of the Holy Spirit I will make the most of opportunities that come my way. May my head be anointed with fresh oil. My path is sure and as the Lord leads me, I will prepare my way before him and achieve all my goals."

My thoughts

_____

_____

_____

_____

_____

STEP OUT...
THEN STAY PUT!

Champions take steps. They step into the unknown by faith. Faith based on the Word. That's how it works. If you have done that, congratulations you are on your way to victory. Now maintain your victory by faith. Such is the victory that overcomes this world system. There is no room for doubt in you! You are an achiever!

And Peter, answering, said to him, "Lord, if it is you, give me the order to come to you on the water."
And he said, "Come." And Peter got out of the boat, and walking on the water, went to Jesus.
But when he saw the wind he was in fear and, starting to go down, he gave a cry, saying, "Help, Lord."

And straight away Jesus put out his hand and took a grip of him, and said to him, "O man of little faith, why were you in doubt?" And when they had got into the boat, the wind went down. (Matt 14: 28-32)

If you've stepped out and it looks a bit boisterous, give Him a shout. He has promised never to leave you nor forsake you. One thing is certain - He'll ensure you don't sink! So circumstances and situations of life cannot possibly put you down. Bounce back! You've got to stop looking at the issues look to the Word! Peter called on the Master (the Word) and had the best stroll of his life. What you have gone through, or are going through becomes immaterial when you call out to him and your hand in His, walk by faith to success and stay put in your victory!

I confess

"...that I will be lead by the Spirit of God always. As I step into the fulfilling of purpose, I do it by faith. Victory is mine. i am focused on the Lord and the Lord of the Word. Nothing can take me out He is my guide, my support and the glory and the lifter up of my head. Thank you Father because with you I can go all the way!"

My thoughts

_____

_____

_____

_____

_____

TAKE RESPONSIBILITY

"Each man is questioned by life; and he can only answer to life by answering for his life; to life he can only answer by being responsible"   Victor Frankl. Since failure entered the world system in Eden, "passing the buck" (making excuses) had been the order of the day.

"It was the woman..." The man had said.

"I didn't mean to, it was the serpent that made me do it..." she explained.

Taking responsibility is fundamental to a successful life. Take God's Word, believe what He says, act on it and change your situations. You are responsible for your actions. This year, every mountain must become a stepping-stone and YOU must see to that! *See to it then that you walk purposefully - not like witless (foolish) creatures, but like wise men."* (Eph. 5:15)

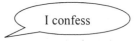

I confess

"...I am a responsible child of God. I take charge of life my walk is purposeful, directed and focused. I am full of wisdom. It is well with me and all that is mine."

PLAN IT...AND MAKE IT!

Jesus said "No king goes to war without proper planning, he needs to know if a thousand men or two will be enough to win the battle." It a less encouraging fact to know that up till now many of us do not have plans or goals for the year.

If you have one, can you run with it? Have you counted the cost? It may need a little fine-tuning. If you must ask for advice, please ask. You may have to study to increase your knowledge base, do that and apply it. Whatever needs to be done to show the glory of God on you - that do!

King Solomon once said, *"Through wisdom is a house built, by understanding it is made stable; and by knowledge shall the rooms be filled with all precious and pleasant riches."* (Proverbs 24:3-4)

I confess

"... and declare the wisdom of God is at work in me. I will walk circumspectly through wisdom, knowledge and understanding. I will achieve as planned by the grace of God."

CALL HIM AND TRUST HIM

Some years ago, I read the story of a man who hung to a rope on a cliff thousands of feet above the sea. As his weary hands began to give way, he cried out, "If there is a God, please help! God please help! I need your help, God!"
Suddenly, it thundered and bright flashes went across the skies, then a voice said,
"Son, my son, I hear you...Let go off the rope..."
"Oh... is anyone else there?" the man cried.

Wrong move...
Friend, faith involves absolute and unreserved trust in the ability of God. Now is the time to trust God to see us through every situation we find ourselves. Arm of flesh is bound to fail, including ours. Faith in God is all we need.

The Word is clear as it says, *"There is no king that is saved by a great army, a mighty man is not delivered by his strength... And it shall come to pass, that whosoever shall call upon the name of the Lord, shall be saved."* (Psalm 32:16, Acts 2:21)
Be encouraged, God is your ready help...call Him...trust Him!

I confess

"...my trust is in the Lord. I believe He is able to uphold me in life and in all I do. I have absolute trust in His protection, grace and kindness to me. He is my Father; my faith is absolute in Him. Thank you Father, you are my saving grace!"

My thoughts

_____

_____

_____

_____

_____

JUST A STEP AWAY...

There is something great about stepping out into the unknown. Just one step with God... births a miracle. When Jesus told Peter to cast his net on the other side, it didn't look like there was going to be a catch. Peter (an experienced fisherman) obeyed the instruction of a carpenter turned preacher. The result was a catch beyond Peter's imagination.

There is great result in obeying God. It's just about believing His Word and acting on it. Elisabeth, Mary's cousin summed it up in Luke 1:45, *"And blessed is she that believed: there shall be a performance of those things which were told her from the Lord."*

And there was!
You are a step away from your next miracle. The secret of having a day-to-day life of miracle is obeying His Word on a day to day basis. As you set out to obey Him, there shall be a performance of what He has told you!

I confess

"...in Jesus name my life is full of the miraculous on a daily basis. Every word of God to me will be fulfilled. I believe, therefore I will see a performance of His promises in my life. My testimony is next!"

My thoughts

_____

_____

_____

_____

_____

SET YOUR FACE!

The rains came, the sun shone for years he remained the same. The other day there was a thunderstorm and strong winds blew he remained the same. He stood there unmoved. His face was set unchanged in heat, cold, winter and summer. Last spring you must have driven past him. I am sure you'll see him same spot when autumn comes. Who else but a statue remains unchanged? Statues don't change! They are always there. They have made up their minds never to be moved. Always focused!

"For the Lord Jehovah will help me; therefore I have not been ashamed. On account of this I have set my face like a flint (statue) and I know that I shall not be ashamed." (Isaiah 50:7)

Focus! That's the word. Make up your mind about your success in life and ministry. Set your face like a statue's! No matter what may be happening around set your mind on succeeding! You can't afford to be double minded. No! The double minded don't receive from the Lord.

In fact, James said, *"Let it not seem to such a man that*

*he will get anything from the Lord; For there is a division in his mind, and he is uncertain in all his ways."(*James. 1: 7-8)

Let the wind blow and the sunshine, your success is sure because the Lord is your help. You have His spirit in you. It may rain cats and dogs He'll see you through as long as set your face on Him and you succeeding. You cannot be ashamed. You will not be ashamed! Focus on His promises; set your face on the Word. Set your face like a flint!

I confess

"...my face is set on my goals. The Lord is my sure help. In my prosperity I shall not be moved. Being double minded is not my portion. My mind is clear, my focus stronger than ever. I will not be put to shame. In Jesus name!"

My thoughts

_____

_____

_____

_____

_____

SOMETHING FOR EVERYONE

The queue was long by the time we got there. Kids giggling with excitement and wishing it was their turn. Parents kept smiles on trying hard not to show the boredom. They had been there and done that! They knew all about it too. But to these little ones there was no going back. They are here at last and Santa Claus is waiting in his grotto. A gift for everyone! Wow!!

"Without faith it is impossible to please Him (God), for those that come to God must believe that he is, and that he is a rewarder of them that diligently seek him." (Hebrews 11:6)

Christmas brings the return of Santa Claus every year. Every one who meets Santa believes he is 'there' and also that no one leaves Santa's presence empty handed.

The anchor of faith lies in the existence of God. *"Only a fool (the simple minded) says (decides) in his heart that there is no God."* Remember, God is real, and He is willing to answer every request you confidently make this year! John confirms this saying, " *And this is the confidence that we have in him, that if we ask any thing according to his will, he heareth us: And if we know that he heareth us, whatever we ask, we know that we have the petitions that we desired from him.* 1 John 5:14 - 15

"...and believe that my God is alive. I am confident that every time I ask according to his will, He hears me. There my prayers are answered, in Jesus name! I look forward to the manifestation of my requests. Thank you Father for you always hear me!"

My thoughts

_____

_____

_____

_____

_____

SITTING ON THE FENCE OR...?

I watched as the cat made its way up the railing, there was a catch on the other side. On the other side was a little pond. A gold fish or two could do for a meal. Thirty minutes down the line he was still on the fence poised ready to leap and catch. Tired of watching, I concluded mummy-cat must have taught him that

"Wrong decision at the Wrong time is a disaster.
Wrong decision at the Right time is a mistake.
Right decision at the Wrong time is unacceptable.
Right decision at the Right time is success"

Life evidently offers us opportunities to make decisions. Friend, sitting on the fence does not bring the meal. Leaping without looking will not bring it either. Life is more than a game. Today is a result of your decisions made yesterday. What will tomorrow look like? Fear not! You can make decisions and get it right. Success is just around the fence. It's all about knowing His will and catching the opportunity at the right time. So Paul encouraged,

"Be most careful then how you conduct yourselves: like sensible men, not like fools. Use the present

opportunity to the full for the days are evil. So be not as fools but try to understand what the will of the Lord is." (Ephesians 5:15-17)

"For as many as are led by the Spirit of God, these are sons of God." (Rom. 8:14)

I confess

"... that as a child of God, His direction to me will be clear. His will for my life is revealed to me by the Holy Spirit. I am led by God's Spirit. I pray in the mighty name of Jesus that on a daily basis, I will continually make right decisions at the right time. Amen."

My thoughts

_____

_____

_____

_____

_____

ONLY BELIEVE!

"I believe God can do anything!" He shouted, "But..."
It's so easy to believe that God can do something for someone, somewhere, some place over six thousand miles away. The truth is revealed when it becomes a personal issue. Yes, everyone believes, but it's high time you faced the truth and settle the fact that God wants to do something for you too.

By the tomb of Lazarus, Martha had her turn, "I know you can do all things BUT he's been buried for four days now," she said.
However, Jesus replied, *"Have I not said to you, that IF you only believe (rely on and trust in me) you will see the glory of God?"* With that he brought Lazarus back to life. (John 11:39-44)

Friend, it is your turn! God wants to do something good in your life too. He is looking for those on whose behalf He will show himself strong. It's time for the manifestation of His glory in your life today - ONLY BELIEVE!

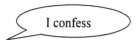

I confess

"...that I am not of them that draw back but of them that stay believer until the day of salvation. Till I see the desires of my heart, I will not give up believing. I know of a surety that my God is working on my behalf. It is my turn my miracle is next!"

My thoughts

_____

_____

_____

_____

SEE THE PRIZE
NOT THE PRICE

The little girl wrote, **"My life as a gold pendant. My beginning was not obvious - I was dark, raw and dirty. Yet I wanted to be the best. One day Mr. Black Smith was not very kind. He put me in hot fire. It was so hot that it burned his finger, but I had to go through it. He also put me on an anvil and hit me many times with a hammer. I still wanted to be the best. Bang, bang, bang and chipping with chisel for many days. But I wanted to be the best. Today, I am a shining gold pendant. Not only that, I am kept in the Queen's jewellery box. Glad to be the best!"**

"Looking unto Jesus, the source and one who perfects our faith. He for the joy that was set before Him, endured the cross, despising and ignoring the shame, and is now seated on the right hand of the throne of God." (Heb. 12:2)

The prize is greater than the price! What you go through cannot be compared to the glory ahead. There is honey in the rock for you. To eat of it you must not consider how your drilling equipment may turn out. Keep your eyes on the perfect example of an achiever Jesus who targeted a heavenly throne, and a kingdom and got it.

The good news is you are not alone. The Greater One who is the source of your faith is with you. His job is also to bring your faith walk to completion desired result. You can fulfil and complete all missions, visions and dreams in style. If you work it the Word way, the end will surely and truly justify the means! Paul rightly said, *"...the Called must eventually be glorified!"* (Rom.8: 30)

I confess

"That I shall be the head and not the tail; that by the help of the Holy Spirit I shall be diligent in all my doings, hardworking and seek to give my best always."

My thoughts

_____
_____
_____
_____
_____

HARVEST IS NEAR

Friend, that's the way it works. Many great things started small. You must keep at it until you get the desired result. Don't be discouraged at all. You have a great future. The Master in a convention meeting laid down an all encouraging thought,

"So is the kingdom of God, as if a man should cast seed into the ground; Go to bed, sleep, and rise night and day, and the seed should spring and grow up, he knows not how."
"For the earth brings forth fruit of herself; first the blade, then the ear, after that the full corn in the ear. But when the fruit is brought forth, immediately he puts in the sickle, because the harvest is come." Mk. 4:26-31

There is nothing wrong with you, your God-given visions, business ideas or goals. It is just normal for things to start small. It's the kingdom way. Be encouraged. Two things can happen to a seed in the soil - either it lives or dies. But because yours is God given - Life given, it will live! Expect it to grow. It will germinate! Keep working at it. Don't give up now.

Mark my words "harvest will come!" It's a kingdom

principle. It will produce fruit! Go get ready for the harvest! *"And though your start was small, your end will be very great."* (Job 8:7)

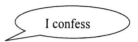
I confess

"My harvest is near. I will enjoy the works of my hand. I expect productivity bountifully harvest from all my labours. My latter end will greater than my start! By my God I will run through a troop and leap over the wall. I see a breaking forth on every side in Jesus name!"

My thoughts

_____

_____

_____

_____

_____

LAUNCH OUT AGAIN...
ONE MORE TIME

The unexpected had happened. Business was closing down. The wave of uncertainty blew in; things were no longer the same. They were left washing nets that caught nothing all night. With boats anchored and out of job for the day, these experienced fishermen could not but their future looking bleak and most uncertain...

The Master turned and said to Simon,
"Launch out into the deep waters, and let down your nets for a draught (haul)."
"Master, we have toiled all the night, and have taken nothing." Simon replied.
"NEVERTHELESS at your word I will let down the net." He added on second thought.
And when they had this done, they hemmed in (wrapped in) a great multitude of fishes: so much that their net began to break. Lk.5:3-7

I am not saying you have not done anything these past months. You have tried, yet nothing has changed. I have good news for you. Your nighttime labour is over. You take Him at his Word. You may not feel like it, but step out on it. It works. You may have failed, yes - that does not make you a failure. Try one more

time. Go back to that vision. Go back to college.
Return to your relationship. Apply for that job again,
this time around backed by His Word. It will work.

Take action now, abundance is around your net.
There is an increase coming your way. Launch out for
a catch!

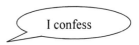

*"...and thank the Lord for his grace and mercy. The
Word works for me! I refuse to be labelled a failure. I
am born of God and have the seed of greatness in me.
Backed by the Word I will succeed in Jesus name."*

My thoughts

_____

_____

_____

_____

_____

FINAL WORDS

"And these all, having obtained a good report through faith, received not the promise: God having provided some better thing for us that they without us should not be made perfect." Heb 11:39 40

By faith the saints of old got outstanding results. Heaven moved on their behalf, rotations of the sun and moon ceased for them. They killed giants, took territories, gave birth against hope, ruled and reigned in high positions without vital qualifications but by favour. It was recorded as a good report.

Now we have been commissioned to go a step further. To perfect their walk, to make it complete, we are to take it to the next level. What a privilege!

God does not waste words. If it was an impossible task for us He would not have entrusted us with the final onslaught on the kingdom of darkness. Every waking day friend should see you walking in victory over the system. You have in you an inherent stamina that overcomes sickness, poverty, lack of direction and death.

Born to win

"For whatsoever is born of God overcometh the world: and this is the victory that overcometh the world, even our faith." 1 John 5:4

If you are born of God all we need to see to declare you victorious is your faith - that state of believing and acting on the Word of God. We don't need to wait till the battle is over. You have won. The victory is your faith because it will always get result. If only we can see faith in you.

Every time Jesus saw faith in someone the next thing he does is to affirm the person's triumph.

"But Jesus turned him about, and when he saw her, he said, Daughter, be of good comfort; thy faith hath made thee whole. And the woman was made whole from that hour." Mat 9:22

"When Jesus saw their faith, he said unto the sick of the palsy, Son, thy sins be forgiven thee." Mar 2:5

Friend, your faith (belief in God's Word and taking the appropriate action) has given you that much needed victory already. You can rejoice in Him. 1 John 5:5 makes known the believer's status.

Who is he that overcometh the world, but he that believeth that Jesus is the Son of God? This should bring peace of mind.

Peace!
Bayo Falode
The Great House, London

OTHER BOOKS BY BAYO FALODE AVAILABLE FROM FAITHOME PUBLICATION

· **Food for Life (vol. 2)**
 T he Walk, The Fight and The Victory
· **Spiritual Growth for Busy People**
 - A practical insight into Christian maturity in our
 ever-demanding world

For more information write to:

Faithome Publications
P.O. Box 410, GRAYS, RM17 9EG
By email: info@faithfeast.com
Tel. 07774965247

 There is great power in the Word of God. The Bible says, "Faith comes by hearing and hearing by the Word of God" Rom.10: 17. Faith the size of a mustards seed will move any mountain that confronts you, so constantly hear and meditate upon God's Word and see your faith grow greatly.

A catalogue of our CDs and Audio tapes is available on request from our office at:

THE GREAT HOUSE MINISTRIES,
2ND FLOOR, BRYSON HOUSE,131 ELM CHURCH LANE,
DAGENHAM, ESSEX, RM10 9RR, UK
TEL:0208 595 7777   MOB: 07917846464
Email:info@thegreathouse.org
Website:www.thegreathouse.org

Bayo Falode pastors The Great House and is the host of "Food for Life". He is a leader with passion and commitment to the kingdom of God. His ministry is blessed with grace, profundity, and the abiding presence of the Holy Spirit with signs following. He encourages walking in the understanding of the principles of God's Word and the practical living a life absolute of victory in God. He travels nationally and internationally, preaching and teaching the Word of God and ministering healing to the sick.

Our Service Times are:

Sunday

TGH ACADEMY CLASSES 10.00AM 10.45AM
WORSHIP SERVICE 11.00AM 1.00PM

Wednesday

BIBLE STUDY 7.30PM 9.00PM

Friday

EVERY FIRST FRIDAY OF THE MONTH
NIGHT OF CHANGE 8.00PM 11.00PM

Contact The Great House

THE GREAT HOUSE MINISTRIES,
2ND FLOOR, BRYSON HOUSE,131 ELM CHURCH LANE,
DAGENHAM, ESSEX, RM10 9RR, UK
TEL:0208 595 7777   MOB: 07917846464
email:info@thegreathouse.org
website:www.thegreathouse.org